THE STATE OF FOOD INSECURITY IN LUSAKA, ZAMBIA

CHILESHE MULENGA

SERIES EDITOR: PROF. JONATHAN CRUSH

Acknowledgements

The author wishes to acknowledge the support of CIDA for funding the AFSUN survey in Lusaka. He also thanks the African Centre for Cities at the University of Cape Town for its support during the tenure of an AFSUN Visiting Fellowship.

Published by the African Food Security Urban Network (AFSUN)
African Centre for Cities, University of Cape Town, Private Bag X3
Rondebosch 7701, South Africa; and Southern African Research Centre,
Queen's University, Canada
www.afsun.org

First published 2013

ISBN 978-1-920597-10-8

Production by Bronwen Dachs Müller, Cape Town

Cover photo by Elizabeth Watkin, PocketCultures, http://bit.ly/HJcOVY

Printed by MegaDigital, Cape Town

AUTHOR

Chileshe Mulenga is a Senior Research Fellow in the Urban Development Research Programme at the Institute of Social and Economic Research, University of Zambia.

Previous Publications in the AFSUN Series

CONTENTS

TABLES

FIGURES

1. INTRODUCTION

Although food insecurity has traditionally been associated with rural areas, it is now increasingly recognized as a serious and growing problem in the cities and towns of Sub-Saharan Africa, where urbanization has not been accompanied by concomitant industrialization and economic growth.[1] Some analysts have observed that poverty and food insecurity in the urban areas of developing countries are seriously underestimated.[2] The policy challenges of ensuring food security in cities and towns characterized by high rates of unemployment and underemployment, informality, overcrowding, deteriorating infrastructure and environmental degradation are formidable. In Zambia, the urban population reached 40% in the 1980s but then stagnated and declined to about 35% by 2000 during a phase of counter-urbanization.[3] Since then, urbanization has resumed its growth trajectory with the urban population doubling between 2000 and 2010. The 2010 Census put the urban population at 39% of Zambia's total population of 13 million (or around 5.1 million urban-dwellers).[4]

Urban population growth in Zambia is likely to maintain its current momentum and keep growing faster than the rural population as national economic growth is predominantly driven by the urban-based sector, especially mining, wholesale and retail trade, and construction. While the national population growth rate was 2.8% per annum between 2000 and 2010, the two largest cities, Lusaka and Kitwe, grew at 4.9% and 3.3% per annum respectively.[5] Zambia's population is also predominantly young (with 53% of the population under 18 years of age) and disproportionately concentrated in urban areas. The demographic composition of the towns and cities favours continued high population growth rates, while the bulk of those born and raised in urban areas can be expected to remain there indefinitely.

Trends in food production and prices in recent years suggest that urban food security in African towns and cities cannot be taken for granted. Africa's low level of agricultural productivity, its increasing dependency on imports to meet its food needs and the fast pace of urbanization are producing serious food security challenges.[6] Low agricultural productivity since the 1960s has resulted in most African countries becoming net food importers. In the case of Zambia, cereals were imported every year from 1986 to 2002.[7] Even though the production of maize (the principal staple crop) improved with the reintroduction of subsidized fertilizers in 2002, it is only in the last three agricultural seasons that national maize production has surpassed production levels in the 1990s. Increased supply and use of fertilizers and hybrid seeds coupled with favourable weather conditions, particularly in the 2009/2010 and 2010/2011 agricultural seasons, led to record agricultural harvests of 2.8 and 1.9 metric tons of maize.[8] On average, however, Zambia meets its national cereal consumption requirements from own production in only one out of every three years.[9]

Food security in Zambia has conventionally been associated with smallholder agricultural production and household poverty in the rural areas.[10] Most of the knowledge and policies for managing food insecurity consequently relate to the rural areas of the country. Such knowledge and experience may not, however, be relevant to the urban areas, because of differences in context and in how the majority of the rural and urban populations access food. For instance, most urban dwellers are net food buyers and depend on food purchases.[11] Above all, access to food in urban areas depends on the availability of food in the market, food prices, and formal and informal incomes.[12] Non-market food transfers from the rural areas can also play a role in mitigating urban food insecurity, but the overall urban food security situation depends on factors other than the supply of food.

Urban agriculture is a feature of the food supply in many African cities and has been advocated as a solution to food insecurity among poor households.[13] In Zambia, there is a large literature on urban agriculture which dates back to the 1980s.[14] Such studies have consistently argued that urban and peri-urban agriculture is all-pervasive in Zambian cities. The 2007-2008 Urban Consumption Survey in Zambia, for example, found that over 85% of households in four cities (Lusaka, Kitwe, Mansa and Kasama) had a food garden.[15] In Lusaka, 40% of households also had a field where they were growing food. Most households were growing vegetables (58%) in their gardens and fields, followed by maize (57%) and fruit (57%). Among poor households (the lowest income tercile), 83% had a food garden and 49% had access to a field. They were also more likely to grow maize and less likely to grow fruit than better-off households. Around 20% of households sold homegrown maize and these households sold 60% of their produce, suggesting a commercial motive for urban agriculture among some households.[16]

Despite the seemingly widespread practice of urban agriculture in Lusaka, various studies have identified numerous obstacles to its further expansion including unsupportive municipal policy, urban expansion and in-filling, land shortages and, most recently, climate change.[17] Some have argued that the urban poor face additional obstacles that make them far less likely to engage in urban agriculture for home consumption and sale.[18] This report focuses on the situation of poor urban households in Lusaka and offers an opportunity to explore this question in greater depth.

Another debate in the Zambian context concerns the nature of urban food supply chains and, in particular, the growing role and impact of modern supermarkets on urban diets and food security.[19] One sub-theme is whether supermarket supply chains offer new market opportunities for small farmers.[20] Supermarkets in Africa initially targeted middle and high-income consumers and the urban middle-class.[21] This might suggest that there is an economic and spatial firewall between supermarkets and poor urban neighbourhoods and households. In other Southern African cities, however, it is clear that supermarkets increasingly figure into the food-sourcing strategies of poor urban households.[22] Supermarkets are also thought to exercise a negative impact on the informal food economy in African cities. However, this view has been contested in the Zambian case. One study has argued, for example, that "'informal' food markets, made up of complex networks of interaction, present a considerable challenge to the claims that supermarkets transform food economies in urban Africa."[23] The data on which this report is based provides insights into both of these contentious issues.

The definition of food security adopted in this report emphasizes the dietary and nutritional aspects of food utilization. In this respect, it builds upon other recent studies of food consumption in Zambia. For example, the Urban Consumption Survey found that wheat had overtaken maize as the most important staple among urban consumers (except among the urban poor) and that urban diets were becoming more diverse.[24] Overall, the survey found that cereals and staples make up 25% of food expenditures, followed by livestock products (21%), fruit and vegetables (18%), and fish and sugar and oils (both 8%).[25] This suggests a relatively diverse diet, although consumption of livestock products, in particular, increased with increased income. This report provides additional insights into the nature and quality of the food security of poor urban households in the informal settlements of Lusaka through the analysis and discussion of the findings of the AFSUN baseline survey of 2008-9.

2. EMERGENCE AND GROWTH OF THE CITY OF LUSAKA

The city of Lusaka emerged at its present location because of its choice as a railway siding in 1905 and subsequent selection as the site for the new colonial capital of Northern Rhodesia in 1931.[26] The development of Lusaka began in earnest in the mid-1930s. While a heavy industrial area and low-cost housing estates for African workers were constructed, its main function remained colonial administration. As a result, growth remained modest until the 1960s. After Zambia's independence in 1964, Lusaka experienced a construction boom that attracted more unskilled and semi-skilled African migrants to the city, exacerbating the acute shortage of low-cost housing and fuelling the growth of squatter and unauthorized settlements.[27]

Over time, Lusaka grew from a small colonial capital and agricultural service centre for surrounding commercial farms into the country's major city, government headquarters and financial, commercial and industrial centre. Comprehensive population statistics for Lusaka are only available from 1963 onwards (Table 1). In 1963, its population was 123,000, which made up 3.5% of the national population and 17% of the urban population (Figure 1). By 2000, the city's population exceeded one million and had increased to 11% of the national population. The growing primacy of Lusaka in the Zambian urban hierarchy over the period meant that by 2000, nearly one-third of Zambia's urban population was in Lusaka. Even during Zambia's decade of so-called counter-urbanization (1990-2000), Lusaka continued to grow at nearly 4% per annum. Between 2000 and 2010, Lusaka added another 600,000 people at an annual growth rate of 5% per annum, raising its share of the overall national population to 17%.

TABLE 1: Population of Lusaka, 1963-2010				
Year	Population	Population growth rate per annum (%)	% of national population	% of urban population
1963	123,146	-	3.5	17.2
1969	262,425	13.4	6.5	22.0
1974	421,000	9.9	9.0	25.3
1980	535,830	4.1	9.4	21.9
1990	769,353	3.7	10.4	26.5
2000	1,103,413	4.0	10.7	31.9
2010	1,742, 979	4.9	17.2	34.4
Sources: Central Statistics Office, Census of Population and Housing 1969, 1974, 1980, 1990, 2000 and 2010				

FIGURE 1: Growth of Lusaka, 1963-2010

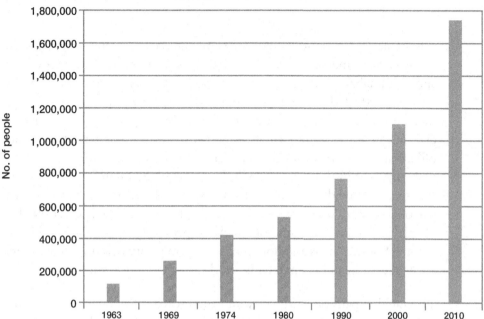

Like most cities in Sub-Saharan Africa, Lusaka was peripheral to the global economy until recently. This is partly due to its inland location and the inward-looking national economic policies that were pursued until the structural and economic reforms of the 1990s. Poor economic performance since the mid-1970s made the city and the country at large unattractive to international capital. However, more recent positive economic trends have led to a marked increase in Foreign Direct Investment (FDI) both in the city of Lusaka and Zambia generally.[28] The financial sector, insurance, real estate and manufacturing have attracted significant FDI into the city. Indian and Chinese investment is also growing rapidly.[29] Lusaka's economy has grown in tandem with its increased roles and functions and it now attracts more investment and people than any other city in Zambia.

Although agriculture and mining are the principal sectors of the national economy, the service sector, along with wholesale and retail trade, are key sectors of the economy of Lusaka, especially in terms of employment generation. Other important sectors of Lusaka's local economy include finance, insurance and real estate, transport and communication, manufacturing, energy, and construction. The city's economic base is set to become even more diverse with the development of the Lusaka East and South Multi-Facility Economic Zones. The construction of these zones has already contributed significantly to the creation of jobs in the construction and related sub-sectors in the city. Once operational, the Multi-Facility Economic Zones will create more jobs in the manufacturing and services sectors, further enlarging Lusaka's contribution to the Zambian economy.

Lusaka already accounts for 50% of Zambia's manufacturing sector (mostly food processing, leather and wood processing, foundries, steel recycling and metal fabrication). It is therefore poised to increase its contribution to the GDP of the country substantially, especially in manufacturing, finance, wholesale and retail trade, and the service sectors. Most financial, insurance and estate agencies and firms in Zambia have their head offices and operations in Lusaka. The services sector is the largest formal employer in the city. The wholesale, retail, and hotel and restaurant sub-sectors provide a significant number of jobs while the provision of personal services is perhaps the largest employer in the city. Over 60,000 people in Lusaka are domestic workers, primarily in high and middle-income housing areas and households. The majority of domestic workers are engaged on an informal basis, working long hours for low wages.

The rapid expansion of the city and the growth of new private housing estates have pushed commercial agricultural activities further away from the city. Agricultural employment around the city has still not recovered from the loss of jobs that followed the collapse of Agriflora in 2005. Agriflora was Zambia's largest producer and exporter of floricultural and horticultural products in the 1990s.[30] The company was based in Lusaka and farmed land on the eastern periphery of the city, providing jobs for women in the low-income and informal housing areas in the north-east and east of the city (especially the residents of Kamanga, Kaunda Square, M'tendere and Chainda). The collapse of Agriflora also led to a general decline of the floricultural and horticultural industry on the eastern peri-urban zones of the city.

Lusaka's built environment is characterized by dramatic contrasts between the formal and informal parts of the city. The formally-developed areas of Lusaka include its central business district, and high, medium and low-cost housing suburbs. Informal parts of the city mainly consist of housing areas that began as squatter or unauthorized settlements and site-and-service schemes. Lusaka's unauthorized settlements were originally located on farms around the city where white farmers had rented land to migrants seeking temporary self-built housing. Squatter settlements, on the other hand, mostly emerged on vacant public property, particularly on land where workers camped during major construction projects.

Two low-cost residential areas were also built on the south-eastern (Chilenje) and southern (Kabwata) edge of the city by the municipal authority. All 37 of the unauthorized and squatter settlements that emerged in Lusaka before and after independence were later upgraded into low-cost high density housing areas. Provision of essential infrastructure and services has remained inadequate in the upgraded settlements, which have high population densities of up to 1,200 persons per hectare. These underserviced areas now account for more than 70% of the city's population and 20% of the built-up area.

The upgrading of squatter and unauthorized housing areas was largely seen as a short-term measure to ease the critical shortage of low-cost housing in the city and improve living conditions. The Housing and Statutory Improvement Areas Act of 1974 provided for the gradual improvement of the settlements by the Ministry of Local Government and Housing. This conferred legal tenure on property owners and led to the extension of essential infrastructure and services, especially transport infrastructure, water supply, and health and education infrastructure.

Informal housing has consequently been the locus of most low-cost housing developments in the city. Prior to the passage of the 1974 Act, shelter was predominantly made of temporary unconventional building materials ranging from uncured soil bricks for walls and plastic, tin, iron and asbestos sheets for roofing. Due to upgrading and provision of secure tenure, squatter housing of this type is no longer part of the city landscape. Most housing in the informal areas is now built from concrete blocks and roofed with either iron or asbestos sheets. The floors are usually unimproved and the dwellings may not have adequate windows and ventilation.

The areas remain extremely overcrowded, which poses serious health risks, especially with regard to communicable diseases.[31] Overcrowded living conditions are worsened by the poor and erratic supply of safe piped water. Although most infrastructure and services were extended to upgraded settlements, the sewerage system was not, mainly on account of the high cost involved. Sanitation is therefore predominantly provided through septic tanks for houses with individual water connections and pit latrines for those without. The water supply and sanitation infrastructure has not grown in tandem with the physical expansion and growing population of the city.

Lusaka's informal economy, in which many of the households in the poor areas of the city participate, grew rapidly in the 1990s during the country's economic crisis and has continued to expand.[32] The majority of Lusaka's youth and adult population now earn livelihoods from informal activities.[33] The informal economy mostly comprises unregistered and unregulated small-scale non-agricultural activities. The majority of people working in the informal economy are self-employed. They are mostly involved in trading activities due to low capital requirements and lower entry barriers. Trading ranges from street vending to trading in the city's central markets, trading areas and markets in the residential areas.[34]

Other informal economic activities include brewing beer (especially so-called "illicit brews"), repair and maintenance of personal and household goods, making goods for sale (such as clothes, knitwear, household furniture and kitchen utensils), sale of second-hand clothing, as well as provision of services such as tailoring, bricklaying, plumbing, electrical works, auto repairs, mining and quarrying, and making and selling building blocks, charcoal and firewood.[35] The majority of the residents of the city engage in several informal economic activities to make ends meet. Participation in informal economic activities is not restricted to those outside the wage economy, but includes those in better-paid formal employment who invest in informal economic activities. Many households in Lusaka therefore engage in multiple livelihood strategies, combining wage employment in either the formal or informal sector with informal economic activities. Renting out property and rooms is another common means of earning income, but is usually done in conjunction with other activities such as wage employment or trading.

Some informal traders cross borders to buy goods from other cities within the region and beyond for resale in Lusaka.[36] Johannesburg, Dar-es-Salaam, Windhoek, Gaborone and Harare are the most popular regional destinations, while Dubai and cities in China and Thailand are emerging as popular international destinations for Zambian traders. Cross-border traders sell directly through rented shops and market stands, as well as through established retailers in the city. Intense competition means low profit margins. Wages in the informal sector tend to be low and often do not enable those who work in the sector to enjoy living standards much above the poverty datum line. The advent of Chinese traders in Zambia is adding to the competition and causing intense local resentment.[37]

3. STUDY METHODOLOGY

Because food insecurity tends to afflict the poorer segments of the population much more than their affluent counterparts, a pro-poor approach was taken in conducting the AFSUN household food security survey in Lusaka. Data on household food security was obtained from a sample survey of Chipata and Mandevu Compounds. These Compounds are located on the northern side of the city and are bounded by the Great North Road in the west and the Ngwerere stream in the south west. Kabanana Site and Service residential area borders Chipata Compound in the north, while Roma Township and Garden Compound lie on the eastern and south eastern flanks of the two townships respectively. They are also traversed by Kasangula Road, which links them to the Great North Road in the west and Roma Township in the east. Chipata and Mandevu Compounds belong to the Mandevu Parliamentary Constituency, one of seven parliamentary constituencies in the city. Mandevu Constituency had a total population of 353,807 in 2010, the second largest constituency in Lusaka after Kanyama. Within Mandevu Constituency, Chipata and Mandevu Compounds account for the bulk of the population, because they host its most populous wards (Raphael Chota, Ngwerere and Justine Kabwe).

A sample of 400 households was selected from Mandevu and Chipata Compounds in August and September 2008. The households were randomly selected by choosing every 10th house along traverses imposed on the two areas. Where the house selected was unoccupied or was a business premises, the next occupied house on the traverse was selected for the interview. Trained interviewers sought to interview the heads of households or other well-informed adults resident in the selected houses. Where the heads of households or informed adults were absent, appointments were made to interview them later in the day. Most of the respondents were either heads of households or close relations such as adult children and spouses.

4. Household Demographic Characteristics

The selected households were made up of 1,978 people of whom 48% were male and 52% female. The mean household size was 4.9 persons although the households ranged from 1 to 16 persons. Two-thirds of the households were relatively small (with 1-5 members) while another 34% had 6-10 household members. Large households with more than 10 members accounted for only 1% of those surveyed. Female-centred households with no male partner made up 21% of those surveyed. This is the lowest proportion of female-centred households of all 11 SADC cities surveyed by AFSUN. Of the remaining households, only 3% were headed by males without a female partner, 28% were extended family households and 48% were nuclear households.

The household heads ranged in age from 18 to 94 with an average age of

38.5. Most of the heads were therefore in their mid to late thirties (Figure 2). The youthfulness of the population in the surveyed areas is seen in the age distribution of household members. Children up to the age of 14 accounted for 42% of the population, while those aged 15-29 accounted for 35%. People aged between 30 and 39 comprised 12% of the population and those 40 years and older only 11%.

FIGURE 2: Age of Household Heads and Members

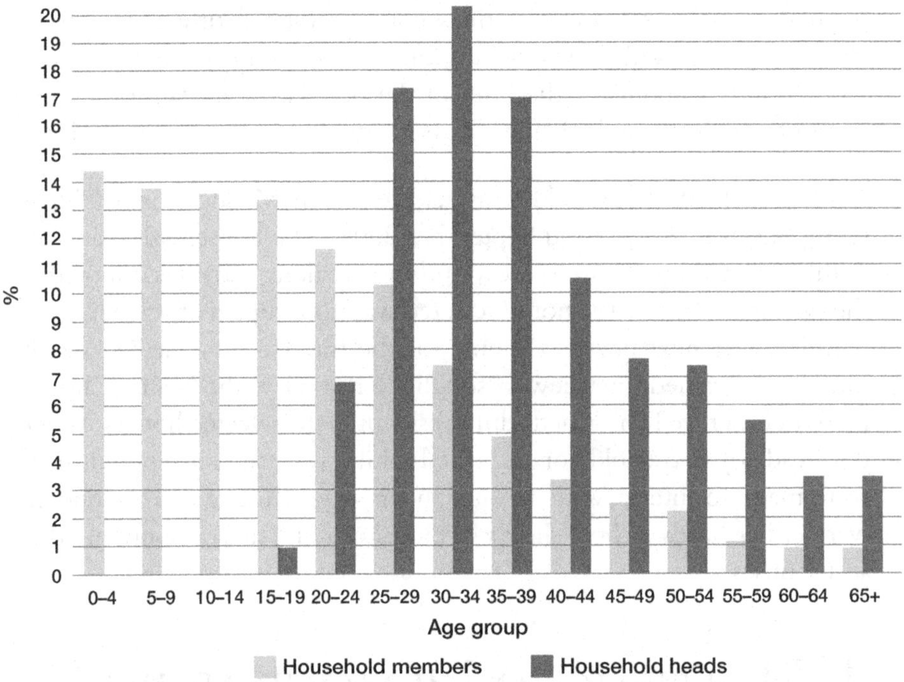

The adult population had low levels of educational attainment: 25% had completed secondary school and only 6% had a post-secondary qualification (just 1% had been to university). This is not surprising given that the compounds were not provided with schools until upgrading began in the 1970s. Children living in the compounds had to walk to the nearest schools in the formal housing areas, and many found it difficult to complete even their primary education. The situation was exacerbated by three decades of economic stagnation when the government introduced cost sharing and user fees in public schools and other services. User fees forced many children out of school as their parents and guardians could not afford to pay them.

The low educational attainment of the adult population consigns them to the lower tiers of the formal labour market or excludes them altogether. Only 35% of the adult population in the surveyed households had full-time formal employment and another 17% were employed part-time or as casual workers. As many as 46% were therefore unemployed, with 15%

performing unpaid housework and only 12% actually looking for work. (Table 2). The largest occupational category was unskilled work (18% of the total adult population and 41% of those in wage employment). At the other end of the spectrum, only 5% of the adult population (and 11% of those in wage employment) were professionals. Nearly half of the working adults were pursuing income-generating activities outside the formal sector: 9% were informal traders and 40% were formal and informal small-scale entrepreneurs. The businesses of the latter ranged from market stands to shops, saloons and roadside businesses (popularly called *tuntemba*.)

TABLE 2: Main Occupations of Adult Population		
	No.	%
Informal/formal entrepreneur	240	40.0
Unskilled worker	112	18.6
Skilled worker	99	16.4
Informal trader	52	8.6
Professional	30	5.0
Office worker/civil servant	15	2.5
Military/security	13	2.1
Employer/manager/supervisor	3	0.5
Farmer/agricultural worker	2	0.3
Other	36	2.2
Total	602	100.0

Most of the members of the surveyed households live and work within the city. However, only 56% of the sample were born in Lusaka. Around 23% were born in rural areas and the rest in other urban areas. The relatively low proportion of rural-urban migrants is consistent with general population trends in Zambia between 1990 and 2000. Poor economic performance led to a marked decline in rural-urban migration, especially of the unskilled and semi-skilled. The 2010 Census, however, indicates a resurgence in the growth of Lusaka over the last decade. Given that the population is predominantly young, much of this growth is probably coming from natural population increase.

5. HOUSEHOLD INCOME AND EXPENDITURE

The main sources of household income are listed in Table 3. Forty-six percent of households derive income from some kind of entrepreneurial activity (with 28% self-classified as informal and 18% as formal). A total of 41% earn income from formal employment and 24% from casual work. Other minor sources of income include cash remittances (15% of households) and rent (13%). Significantly, less than 1% of the households obtain income from the sale of either rural or urban agricultural produce. Average income from most sources is low and uneven, which helps explain why many households rely on more than one source. Average income from wage work, for example, is K600,000 per month (just over USD2,000 per annum at the 2008 exchange rate), which is lower than average earnings from both formal and informal entrepreneurial activity. Average household income from remittances, casual work and rent is lower still. While average income from other sources is not insignificant, the number of household beneficiaries is extremely small.

TABLE 3: Sources of Household Income

	No. of households	% of households	Monthly average income (Kwacha)	Average annual income (USD)
Wage work	165	41.2	599,528	2,055
Informal business	112	28.0	672,803	2,306
Casual work	95	23.7	249,571	856
Formal business	72	18.0	820,461	2,813
Remittances	62	15.5	369,905	1,268
Rent	54	13.5	187,704	644
Rural farm products	4	0.1	437,500	1,500
Urban farm products	4	0.1	333,333	1,142
Aid	2	<0.1	60,000	206
Pension	3	<0.1	750,000	2,571
Other	2	<0.1	100,000	343
Note: Multiple response question				

Income inequality in the surveyed households was very high. While the average monthly income of the surveyed households was just under K900,000, at least 50% earn less than K520,000 per month. Inequality was most pronounced among those earning incomes from informal and formal business activity and less pronounced among those earning income from wage employment. Other highly skewed incomes occurred among the households that relied on remittances and rental incomes. Households that relied on remittances and casual employment reported some of the lowest monthly incomes (of less than K10,000 per month).

As noted above, many households obtain income from more than one source. Only 25% of households had no source of income other than wage employment. Another 48% had one or two additional sources (24%

each). Sixteen percent had three additional sources and 10% had four or more. Households with one additional livelihood strategy were mainly reliant on marketing (32%), renting to lodgers (22%), self-employment at home (25%) and the provision of casual labour (15%). The 50% of households that relied on multiple livelihood activities tended to be involved in the same activities. A striking finding is that households with wage income were not entirely dependent on this source. While this is partly because many jobs pay very low wages, wage employment also provides earners with capital to engage in buying and selling or marketing.

Further insights into the welfare challenges faced by surveyed households can be obtained from scrutiny of their expenditures. Table 4 shows the proportion of households that incurred expenditures on a particular expense category in the month prior to the survey. Over 90% of households spent income on food, easily the highest expenditure category. Over 70% incurred expenses on basic services (shelter, electricity and fuel). Half of the households had spent money on children's education. One in five households incurred medical expenses and sent remittances (probably to relatives in the rural areas). The incomes of most of the households surveyed were so low that over 90% could not save anything. Food was the single biggest household expenditure item (averaging K273,241 or USD78 per month) followed by housing, fuel, utilities and education. Expenditures on food made up 47% of the total spend of all households, far greater than any other category.[38] Housing was next (at 16%) followed by fuel (8%), utilities (8%) and education (5%).

TABLE 4: Household Expenditures				
	No.	% of households	Average monthly expenses	% of expenditures by all households
Food and groceries	362	90.5	K273,241	47.0
Fuel	312	78.0	K56,995	8.4
Utilities	311	77.8	K52,754	7.8
Housing	280	70.0	K122,312	16.3
Education	219	54.8	K50,165	5.2
Medical expenses	92	23.0	K11,321	0.5
Remittances	87	21.8	K40,911	1.7
Transportation	80	20.0	K112,850	4.3
Debt service/repayment	43	10.8	K34,452	0.7
Goods purchased to sell	33	8.3	K261,888	4.1
Funeral costs	18	4.5	K33,681	0.3
Savings	15	3.8	K457,000	3.3
Home-based care	4	1.0	K40,625	<0.1
Note: Multiple response question				

Housing expenses reflect disparities in both incomes and housing quality. Although the average monthly spend on housing was K122,000, at least 50% of the households spent less than K95,000 per month. Most of these households rented rooms in very poor quality houses with communal toilets and water taps. Other households that paid more than the monthly average generally rented houses or flats with individual toilets, but were unlikely to have individual water connections. They therefore rely on communal water taps for their water supplies. The smaller number who paid more than K500,000 per month were more likely to be in houses with individual water connections and water-borne toilets connected to septic tanks.

6. FOOD SOURCING IN LUSAKA

6.1 Formal and Informal Food Purchase

A rounded picture of food sourcing in Lusaka can be obtained by combining the findings of the AFSUN survey with the 2007-2008 Urban Consumption Survey conducted in four Zambian cities by Michigan State University.[39] The Urban Consumption Survey asked a representative sample of households in Lusaka where they had purchased their food staples (wheat, sorghum, millet and cassava flour, maize meal, rice, samp, pasta, bread, sugar, cassava and potatoes) in the previous month. There were several key findings:

- Only 12% of all households had bought staples at supermarkets.
- The patronage of supermarkets consistently increased as household income rose. Only 1% of households in the lowest income quintile bought staples at supermarkets compared with 28% in the upper income quintile (Table 5).
- Most households (44%) bought staples from small outlets such as grocers, small shops and bakeries.
- The patronage of small shops decreased with increased income from 50% of households in the lowest quintile to 35% in the upper quintile.
- Patronage of the informal food economy was also significant at 42% of all households.
- With the exception of households in the upper quintile, the relationship between income and patronage of the informal economy was not strong.

The Urban Consumption Survey suggests that overall supermarket penetration of the food retail market is relatively low in Lusaka except among higher-income households. But even there, the majority (70%) still do not buy staples at supermarkets.

TABLE 5: Sources of Staple Foods by Household Income						
	Income Quintiles (% of households)					Total
	1 (Low)	2	3	4	5 (High)	
Supermarkets	1	5	6	14	28	12
Informal vendors	46	43	45	42	35	42
Grocers/shops/bakeries	50	49	46	44	36	44
Source: Mason and Jayne, "Staple Food Consumption" p. 18.						

The purchasing pattern for livestock products differed from that for staples (Table 6):[40]

- 8% of households bought meat from supermarkets and 25% from informal vendors. The vast majority of Lusaka households (64%) purchased their meat from butcheries.

- As with staples, the patronage of supermarkets increased with income (from 1% of households in the lowest income tercile to 18% of those in the upper tercile).

- Patronage of butcheries was relatively consistent across the income terciles, although those in the lowest tercile made much greater use of informal sources of meat.

- The informal economy was the major supplier of chicken and poultry (73%) with only 8% buying chicken at supermarkets. However, better-off households tended to make less use of the informal economy and more use of supermarkets (55% and 19% respectively).

- Fish sales were completely dominated by the informal economy but this too is related to income (with 91% of low-income households and 57% of higher-income households obtaining fish in this manner).

- The informal economy is the most popular source for dairy products such as eggs (70%) and milk (52%), although grocers are also an important source for many households.

TABLE 6: Sources of Meat, Chicken and Dairy				
	Percentage of households			
	Meat	Chicken	Eggs	Milk
Supermarkets	8	8	6	9
Grocers	2	4	19	33
Butcheries	63	4	1	2
Informal sources	25	73	70	52
Other	2	11	4	4
Source: Hichaambwa, "Urban Consumption Patterns of Livestock Products", pp. 13-16.				

The Urban Consumption Survey showed that the informal food economy (markets stalls, mobile and street vendors, and small informal shops or kiosks) is the major source of most foods for lower-income households. Meat is the only exception, as it is primarily obtained from local butcheries. Supermarket patronage is minimal, even for the purchase of staples.

The AFSUN survey corroborates the Urban Consumption Survey finding for Chipata and Mandevu Compounds. Rather than asking where households had obtained particular foodstuffs during the previous month, the AFSUN survey asked where households "normally" obtained food (more than one answer was permitted) and how often they patronized each source. Ninety-one percent of the households reported that they obtained food from the informal food economy and 73% that they bought from small shops (Table 7). Only 14% said they patronized supermarkets.

TABLE 7: Formal and Informal Economy as Sources of Food		
Source of food	No.	%
Informal market/street food	365	91.3
Small shop	292	73.0
Supermarket	57	14.3
Note: Multiple response question		

The dominance of informal markets and small shops as sources of food can be partially attributed to the fact that there were no supermarkets in the study area while informal vendors and small shops were commonplace. These outlets provide food in small, affordable quantities, which enable households to buy on a daily basis. The vast majority of households in the survey (92%) reported that they purchased food from informal sources at least five days a week. Another 7% did so once a week. Nearly half of the households (48%) reported buying food from small shops at least five days a week and another 25% at least once a week.

The main reason for daily food shopping is that many poor urban households in Lusaka depend on casual employment and informal trading and vending for income. The income flow is unreliable and erratic and therefore they cannot afford to buy food in bulk or in advance. Food is bought as and when money becomes available and in affordable quantities. Supermarkets tend to sell food in larger quantities, which most poor households simply cannot afford. For example, while better-off households in Lusaka buy maize meal from supermarkets in 25kg bags, the less well off buy the same commodity from informal markets and small shops in packets weighing between 500g and 1kg. These small packets of maize meal are popularly called *tu Pamela*, a name that suggests they were popularized by single young women with unstable incomes living on their own.

6.2 Other Food Sources

In Chipata and Mandevu Compounds there appears to be very little participation in urban agriculture. Only 10 of the randomly surveyed households in the study area (or 3%) reported that they grew any of their own food and just seven (2%) that they derived any income from the sale of home-grown food. It is unlikely that even these households were growing their food within the city itself.

Informal food transfers from relatives and friends in rural areas and other urban areas proved to be a more significant source of food in many of the cities surveyed by AFSUN.[41] Around one in four (or 26%) of the households reported receiving food from relatives in the rural areas and another 4% reported receiving food from other urban areas. Some respondents received food transfers from both rural and urban areas, while others received food only from one or the other. For example, 39% of recipient households received food only from the rural areas, 44% from other urban areas only and 17% from both rural and urban areas.

The types of food received from rural and other urban areas do not differ significantly (Table 8). In both cases, cereals are the most common food received (with 23% of households receiving cereals from other urban areas and 21% from rural areas). In effect, this means that almost all of the one in four households receiving transfers get cereals. Maize, which is milled and then cooked into maize meal (*nshima*), was undoubtedly the dominant cereal. Second most important were vegetables (around 11% of total households) followed by foods made from beans, peas, lentils or nuts (which were twice as likely to come from rural than other urban areas). Less than 10% of households received food from any of the other major food groups.

TABLE 8: Types of Food Transferred to Lusaka		
	Rural %	Urban %
Cereals (foods made from grains)	20.6	23.0
Foods made from beans, peas, lentils, or nuts	14.4	7.0
Vegetables	11.2	11.5
Roots or tubers	9.7	3.4
Meat, poultry or offal	7.0	5.0
Fresh or dried fish or shell fish	2.6	5.7
Fruits	1.3	2.9
Foods made with oil, fat, or butter	0.3	2.1
Sugar or honey	0.3	3.1
Cheese, yoghurt, milk or other milk products	0.0	0.8

Examination of the frequency of food transfers from rural and urban areas showed distinct differences between the two. Rural-urban food transfers are relatively sporadic with less than 3% of transfers occurring regularly (every week) and over two-thirds occurring infrequently (just once a year). This suggests that rural-urban transfers are neither regular nor reliable and can only be depended on occasionally to mitigate food insecurity. Less than 1% of the recipient households considered the food transfers critical to their survival, suggesting that the transfers may have more to do with maintaining social ties than food security. In the case of urban to urban food transfers, the pattern is reversed with most transfers (particularly of cereals and vegetables) occurring relatively frequently (monthly or weekly). These food transfers were seen as important to survival by 53% of the recipient households. In urban Zambia, it is not uncommon for better-off households to support less well-off relatives or to have their own dependents living in low-income or informal housing areas. Urban-urban food transfers therefore play a much more important role than urban agriculture in the food security of households.

TABLE 9: Frequency of Food Transfers				
	Cereals (%)	Roots/tubers (%)	Vegetables (%)	Beans/lentils/peas/nuts (%)
Rural-Urban				
Often	1	3	0	2
Regular	8	6	13	9
Occasional	23	17	18	22
Infrequent	68	75	70	67
Urban-Urban				
Often	25	15	37	18
Regular	56	23	51	48
Occasional	11	39	7	11
Infrequent	7	23	4	18

Most of the households surveyed did not obtain food through formal or informal social protection channels (Table 10). Only 3-5% of households obtained food through sharing with neighbours or borrowing from neighbours. This is because most residential areas in Lusaka, including the low-income compounds, are highly heterogeneous and neighbours mostly do not share any social or kinship ties, such as speaking the same mother tongue or originating from the same district or region. As a result, most households strive to be as independent of other households as they can, except in times of crisis or emergency when neighbours do feel obliged to provide some relief.

Community food kitchens were not relied on by any of the households (bar one), mainly because they are not available or provided by any agency in Lusaka. In part this may be due to the low prevalence of destitute groups, such as the homeless and street children, which encourage charitable groups in cities elsewhere to provide such services. When there was a street-children crisis in the late 1990s and early 2000s, food kitchens and drop-in centres were provided in Lusaka, but they targeted the central business district and other commercial areas where the street children tended to live or operate from. Few of the street children lived in residential neighbourhoods such as the study area even if they originated from there. Only two of the households received any food aid, probably in the form of supplementary food given to persons living with HIV/AIDS and tuberculosis.[42]

TABLE 10: Other Sources of Food		
	No.	%
Shared meal with neighbours	46	5.1
Food provided by neighbours and/or other household	36	4.0
Borrow food from others	30	3.3
Food aid	2	0.2
Community food kitchen	1	0.1
Note: Multiple response question		

7. HOUSEHOLD FOOD INSECURITY

According to the 1996 World Food Summit, food security is a state "when all people at all times have physical, social and economic access to sufficient, safe and nutritious food that meets their dietary needs and food preferences for an active and healthy life". This universally-accepted definition of food security clearly indicates that it is a complex and multi-dimensional concept encompassing three main elements: availability, access and utilization of food. Each of these elements is usually measured with different tools and at different scales. The availability of food is often measured at the national level with the help of food balance sheets.[43] The utilization of food is measured at the individual level with the help of anthropometric indices such as wasting and stunting.[44]

Access to food has been the most difficult element to measure and quantify. Data on caloric adequacy, for example, is not only technically challenging to collect but labour intensive and costly. The success of the Household Food Security Survey Module – used and validated for assessments of access to food at the household level in the United States – has inspired new tools based on the idea that the experience of food insecurity arouses predictable reactions and responses in individuals.[45] A number of tools focused on the experience of food insecurity and the reactions it elicits have therefore been developed.[46]

AFSUN chose the measures developed by the Food and Nutrition Technical Assistance Project (or FANTA). These measures are easy to implement, can be adapted to different socio-economic settings and have been successfully used in many African countries. They include the following:

- Household Food Insecurity Access Scale (HFIAS): The HFIAS measures the degree of food insecurity during the month prior to the survey. An HFIAS score is calculated for each household based on answers to nine food consumption-related "frequency-of-occurrence" questions.[47] The minimum score is 0 and the maximum is 27. The higher the score, the more food insecurity the household experienced.

- Household Food Insecurity Access Prevalence Indicator (HFIAP): The HFIAP indicator uses the responses to the HFIAS questions to group households into four levels of household food insecurity: food secure, mildly food insecure, moderately food insecure and severely food insecure.

- Household Dietary Diversity Scale (HDDS): Dietary diversity refers to how many food groups were consumed within the household in the previous 24 hours.[48] The FAO classification for Africa identifies 12 distinct food groups. The scale therefore ranges from a minimum of 0 to a maximum of 12. An increase in the average number of different food groups consumed provides a quantifiable measure of improved household food access.

- Months of Adequate Household Food Provisioning Indicator (MAHFP): The MAHFP indicator captures changes in the household's ability to ensure that food is available above a minimum level throughout the year.[49] Households are asked to identify in which months (during the past 12 months) they did not have access to sufficient food to meet their household needs. The MAHFP scores range between 0 ("never enough food") and 12 ("always enough food"). The scale is incremental: as the score increases, so does adequate food provisioning.

These measures make it possible to capture and quantify with confidence the levels of access to food in any population by measuring the feelings of uncertainty or anxiety sparked by food insecurity. Analysis of food quality and quantity also make it possible to ascertain the diversity of the diet. These tools also provide insights into the temporal aspects of access to food. The rest of this section presents the findings on food security in the low-income households of the surveyed compounds in Lusaka.

7.1 Food Access

The average HFIAS score for the households was 11.5 out of 27 (Table 11). The Lusaka score was worse (i.e. higher) than six of the other cities surveyed by AFSUN (Blantyre, Cape Town, Gaborone, Johannesburg, Windhoek and Maputo) and better than only three (Harare, Manzini and Maseru, all of which have particularly acute food insecurity). Half of the households had scores over 11 and a quarter had scores over 15, indicating intense food insecurity. Only 4% of the households had scores of 0, indicating complete food security.

Table 11: HFIAS Scores			
HFIAS	No.	% of total	Cumulative %
0	17	4.4	4.4
1	3	0.8	5.2
2	3	0.8	6.0
3	6	1.6	7.6
4	8	2.1	9.7
5	14	3.6	13.3
6	25	6.5	19.8
7	26	6.7	25.5
8	18	4.7	30.2
9	32	8.3	38.5
10	18	4.7	42.2
11	25	6.5	48.7
12	19	4.9	53.6
13	24	6.2	59.8
14	23	6.0	65.8
15	24	6.2	71.9
16	23	6.0	77.9
17	18	4.7	82.6
18	25	6.5	89.1
19	11	2.8	91.9
20	4	1.0	92.9
21	9	2.4	95.3
22	2	0.5	95.8
23	5	1.3	97.1
24	3	0.8	97.9
25	1	0.3	98.2
26	0	0.0	
27	0	0.0	

The HFIAP was used to categorize the surveyed households into four different food insecurity classes. Table 12 shows the different levels of food insecurity among the surveyed households. Only 4% of the households fell into the totally food secure category and another 3% were mildly food insecure. Nearly a quarter of the households (24%) were moderately food insecure and over two-thirds (69%) were severely food insecure. Some AFSUN studies combine the latter two categories into a single "food insecure" class.[50] If this exercise is done with the Lusaka data, 92% of households count as food insecure. Only crisis-ridden Harare, of all the cities surveyed, has a higher prevalence of food insecurity.

TABLE 12: Household Food Insecurity Categories	
	%
Food secure	4.4
Mild food insecurity	3.4
Moderate food insecurity	23.6
Severe food insecurity	68.7

7.2 Dietary Diversity

The HDDS throws light on the diversity of the foods eaten within the household. Households that consumed foods from many different groups are awarded higher scores to a maximum of 12. A zero score indicates that no food was consumed at all in the household in the previous 24 hours. The average HDDS score for the surveyed households was 4.8. Forty-five percent of the households had a score of 4 or less and 61% a score of 5 or less (Table 13). This compares unfavourably with the AFSUN database for 11 SADC cities where the equivalent figures were 34% (4 or less) and 48% (5 or less). In addition, no Lusaka households had a score of 10 or higher (compared with 10% of the regional sample). This means that the Lusaka sample has a significantly less diverse diet than other poor households in the region. Most households surveyed in Lusaka ate a very narrow range of foods. Nearly 80% only consumed half of the types of food that should be eaten to ensure a balanced diet.

The narrow range of food in the average household diet is clear from data on which food groups were eaten from in the previous 24 hours (Table 14). The three most common food types (consumed in at least 50% of the households) were cereals (93%), vegetables (80%) and sugar (62%). The majority of households had not consumed roots and tubers, beans and nuts, fruit, eggs, milk products, meat, poultry or fish. These findings are consistent with the fact that most of the poor population relies heavily for nourishment on cereals in the form of cooked maize meal (*nshima*) eaten with a few vegetables as relish. Around a third of the households, especially those with higher incomes, added meat or poultry and fresh or dried fish to their main meal. The low consumption of legumes was surprising as beans are known to be the main source of protein for poor households in Zambia as a whole. However, dry beans are usually purchased by households, take a long time to cook and consume a lot of cooking fuel, which could explain the low consumption in these poor households. Sugar was mostly used in beverages, especially tea and coffee, which might be consumed with bread and other wheat products in the morning for breakfast, or even as lunch for households that could not afford two main meals of *nshima* with relish.

TABLE 13: Household Dietary Diversity

HDDS	Lusaka %	Lusaka cumulative %	Region %	Region cumulative %
0	1	1	0	0
1	2	3	2	2
2	16	19	11	13
3	12	31	10	23
4	14	45	11	34
5	16	61	14	48
6	18	79	13	61
7	8	87	12	73
8	9	96	10	83
9	4	100	7	90
10	0		4	94
11	0		3	97
12	0		3	100

TABLE 14: Types of Foods Consumed

	Yes %	No %
Cereals (foods made from grains)	93.2	6.8
Vegetables	79.9	20.1
Sugar or honey	62.0	38.0
Foods made with oil, fat, or butter	43.8	56.2
Fresh or dried fish	33.1	66.9
Meat or poultry or offal	26.8	73.2
Foods made from beans, peas, lentils, or nuts	25.7	74.3
Eggs	18.4	81.6
Fruits	17.7	82.3
Cheese, yoghurt or other milk products	12.8	87.2
Roots and tubers	12.6	87.4
Other foods	61.3	38.7
Note: Multiple response question		

The diet of the majority of households was therefore deficient in most essential nutrients, especially proteins, minerals and vitamins. In the 1990s, the situation in Zambia was so bad that some vitamin and mineral deficiencies were declared public health hazards (including vitamin A and iron and iodine deficiencies).[51] To address these deficiencies in the Zambian diet, the government imposed vitamin A and iodine fortification in sugar and salt respectively to improve their intake in the country. The sale of unfortified sugar and salt was prohibited. In addition, pregnant women were given iron supplements at antenatal clinics to reduce the risk of anaemia during pregnancy.

7.3 Months of Adequate Food Provisioning

The MAHFP sheds light on whether access to food in urban areas is subject to seasonal fluctuations. Food price spikes often occur a few months before the next harvest when food stocks are low, especially in the absence of adequate strategic food reserves. In rural areas, the seasonal fluctuations in food supply are reflected in the "hunger months", three to four months before the harvest season.[52] Eighty-five percent of the surveyed households in Lusaka said that they experienced months of inadequate food provisioning (Table 15). Only 15% of the surveyed households had a score of 12, however. Sixty-three percent of households had scores between 9 and 11. The remaining 22% had four or more months of inadequate food supply.

TABLE 15: Months of Adequate Household Food Provisioning			
	No.	%	Cumulative %
0	8	2.0	2.0
1	0	0.0	2.0
2	1	0.3	2.3
3	4	1.0	4.3
4	2	0.5	4.8
5	9	2.3	7.1
6	9	2.3	9.4
7	22	5.6	15.0
8	32	8.1	23.1
9	73	18.6	41.7
10	97	24.7	66.4
11	78	19.8	85.2
12	58	14.8	100.0

January and February were the only months when more than 50% of the households had enough food to eat (Figure 3). By March the proportion dropped to 34% and fell to a low of 10 in October. From April to July less than 20% of the households had enough food to eat. Although the proportion rose to 22% in August it dropped again in September. More than half of the households therefore did not have enough food to eat in 10 out of the previous 12 months. Urban households have 10 "hunger months" to contend with, unlike their rural counterparts for whom the hunger months are usually confined to three to four months before the harvest.

FIGURE 3: Level of Adequate Food Provisioning by Month

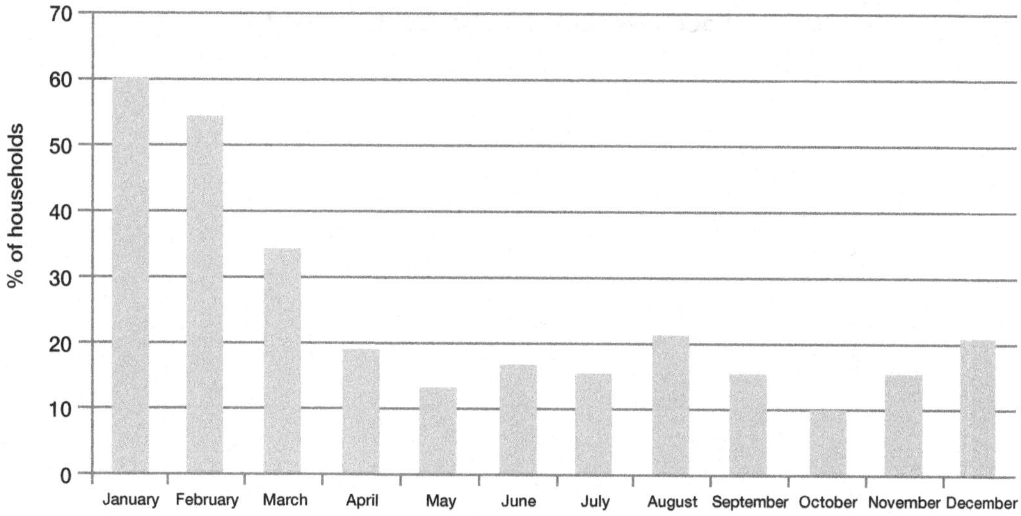

8. DRIVERS OF HOUSEHOLD FOOD INSECURITY

The socio-economic characteristics of the surveyed households have a bearing on access to food at household and individual levels. These include household structure, size, income, employment status and poverty. This section examines the association of these variables with mean household food security status using the FANTA indicators, commenting mainly on those cases where there is a strong statistical relationship.

8.1 Food Security and Household Structure

How does food security status relate to household structure? Of the four major types of household, female-centred households were the most food insecure with an average HFIAS of 12.7 (Figure 4). They were followed by extended family households with 11.5. The male-centred and nuclear households were the least food insecure with scores of 9.6 and 10.9

respectively. Thus, household structure has a strong association with food insecurity, especially in terms of access to food. Female-centred households were clearly the most food insecure and also had the lowest dietary diversity scores with a mean of 4.5 (Figure 5). Male-centred households scored 5.1, nuclear households 5.0 and extended households 4.9. This means that female-centred households not only find it the most difficult to access food, they also have the least diverse diets and are therefore most vulnerable to macro and micro-nutrient deficiencies.

FIGURE 4: Food Insecurity and Household Structure

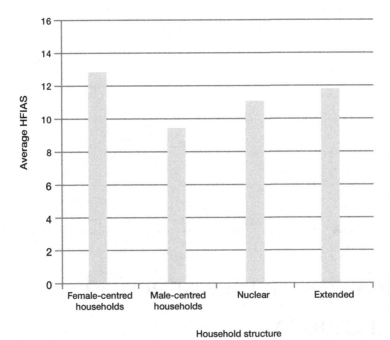

FIGURE 5: Dietary Diversity and Household Structure

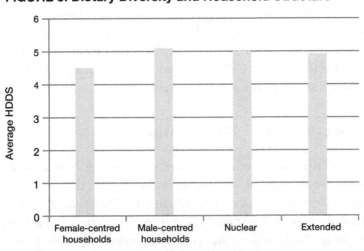

Another way of looking at the relationship between gender and food security is to differentiate between all households with a female head and all those with a male head of household. What this analysis shows is that male-headed households have better access to food and higher household dietary diversity than their female counterparts (Figure 6). The primary reason for this finding is that male-headed households tend to have higher incomes due to higher participation rates of men in the better-paying formal sector. While men dominate formal sector employment, women tend to be relegated to low-income employment and unprotected informal-sector jobs. Male-headed households would therefore be expected to have better access to food, both in terms of quantity and quality.

FIGURE 6: Food Insecurity and Sex of Household Head

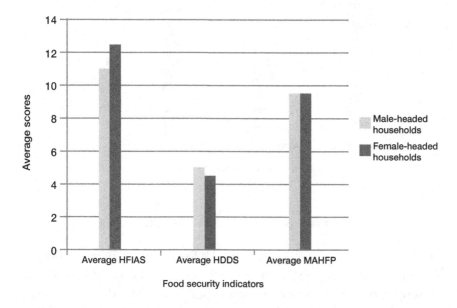

8.2 Food Security and Household Size

There is a clear relationship between household size and food access and dietary diversity. The larger the household the more food insecure it is. The largest households (>10 members) have the highest average HFIAS scores (12.3) and the lowest HDDS (4.3). The association of large households with inadequate access to food and lower household dietary diversity is in line with the findings of poverty assessments undertaken in Zambia, which show that the larger extended family households tend to be poorer than small and medium-size households. There are at least two anomalies in the relationship between household size and food insecurity. First, households with 6-10 members tend to be more food secure on the HFIAS than those with only 1-5 members. This is probably because the former are more likely to have more than one adult income earner. However, this does not mean that they have more diverse diets. Second, the largest households actually have a slightly higher MAHFP score than medium and smaller households. This means that, on average, they report more months of food adequacy.

FIGURE 7: Food Insecurity and Household Size

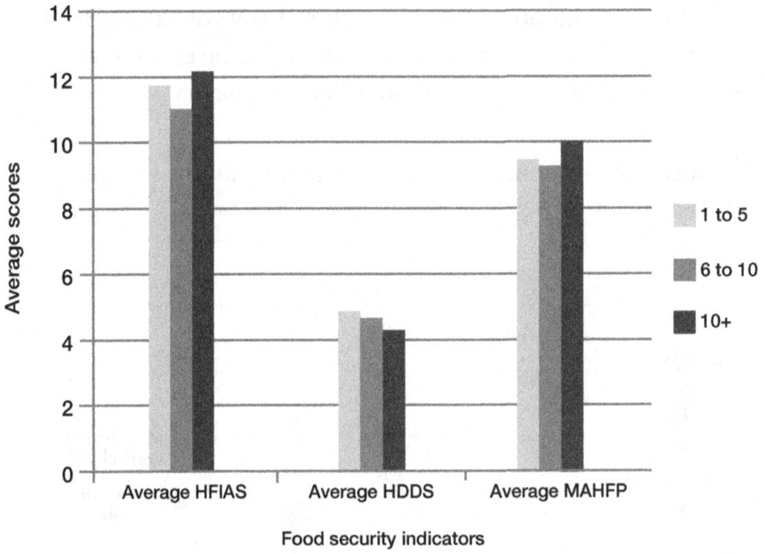

8.3 Food Security and Household Income

Income usually has a strong bearing on the food security of urban households, particularly because they depend almost entirely on markets for their food supply. In a setting where the vast majority of the food consumed has to be purchased, and where household income is low and unpredictable, a strong relationship ought to exist between levels of household income and food security. The survey showed that even within poor communities, higher-income households had better access to food, higher household dietary diversity and more months of adequate household food provisioning. Similarly, middle-income households had better access to food, higher household dietary diversity and more months of adequate household food provisioning than the lowest-income households.

Another reason why access to income is a major determinant of household food security in Lusaka is because poor urban households do not receive as much in informal food transfers from rural areas as those in other Southern African cities. This is mainly due to weak rural-urban links and the tendency for many households to move to the cities and towns on a permanent basis, resulting in less motivation for maintaining ties with the rural areas. Very high levels of poverty and rural-urban poverty disparities also mean that rural households can only afford to send small quantities of surplus production to the cities in the immediate post-harvest period.

FIGURE 8: Food Insecurity and Household Income

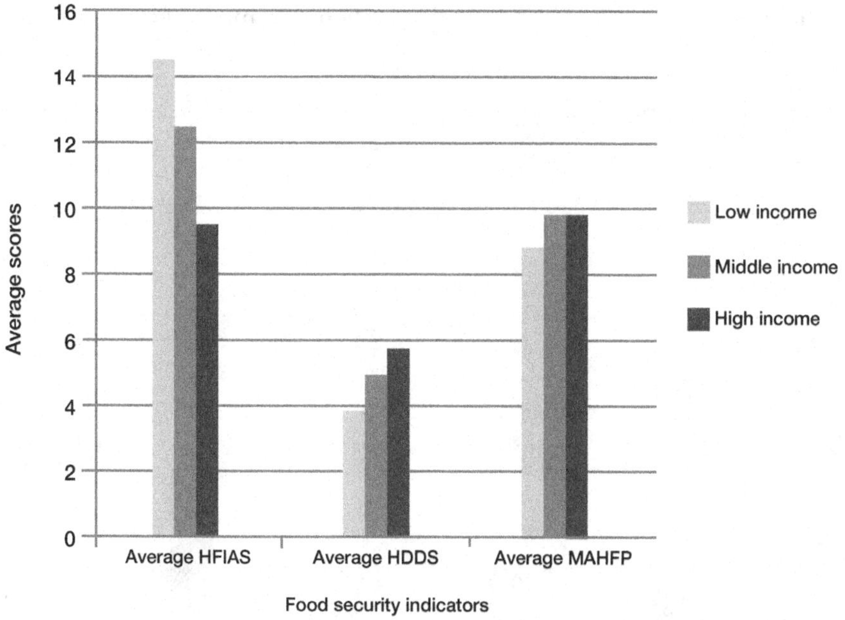

8.4 Food Security and Poverty

The Living Conditions Monitoring Survey (LCMS) published by the Central Statistical Office uses a food poverty line to determine levels of urban poverty in Zambia.[53] Although, the survey claims there was a drop in poverty prevalence from 56% in 2004 to 34% in 2006, such claims have been contested by NGOs and researchers. The LCMS methodology has been heavily criticized for underestimating the extent of urban poverty by failing to take into account the high cost of non-food needs.[54] As a result, the AFSUN study avoided using the LCMS figures for poverty levels in Lusaka. Instead, it used the Lived Poverty Index, based on household responses to five "frequency-of-occurrence" questions as a quantifiable measure of household poverty.[55]

The questions seek to establish how often households have gone without various basic needs including food, clean water for home use, fuel for cooking, medicine or medical treatment and cash income over the previous six months. The proportion of households that had never had to do without ranged from 6% for cash income, 11% for adequate cooking fuel, 12% for enough food, 21% for medicine or medical treatment and 28% for clean water (Figure 9). This means that only a minority of households had not gone without any of these basic needs. Most households (between 72% and 94%) had to do without all five basic needs at least once or twice. Households that had gone without many times or always included 30% for income, 20% for enough food, 16% for enough clean water, 11% for adequate cooking fuel and 10% for medicine or medical treatment.

FIGURE 9: Lived Poverty in Lusaka

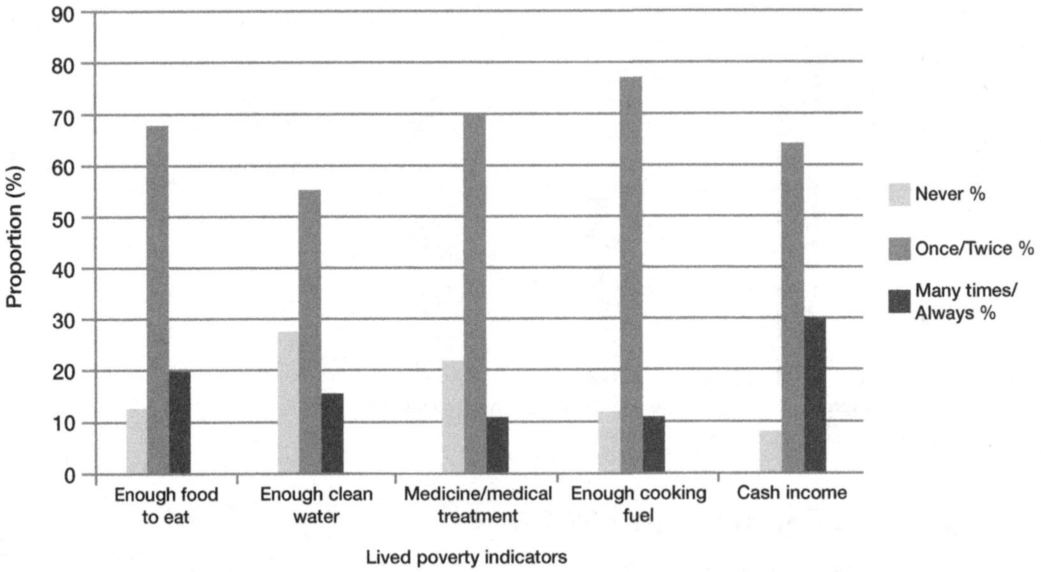

To assess the association between poverty and household food security, we used the Lived Poverty Index and the three food insecurity indicators. There proved to be a strong positive relationship between the Lived Poverty Index categories and the indices of food insecurity (Figure 10). Least poor (never without) households had better access to food and higher household dietary diversity scores, as well as more months of adequate household food provisioning. The poorest (often or always without) households had the worst access to food, lower household dietary diversity scores and the lowest months of adequate household food provisioning. The food insecurity scores of the middle category (sometimes without) fell in-between.

The association between poverty and food insecurity is not surprising, since both tend to be influenced by income levels. Urban poverty assessments have repeatedly shown that households that depend on incomes from protected formal employment tend to be the least poor, while those earning incomes from the unprotected informal sector tend to be poorest. The amelioration of both poverty and food insecurity is therefore closely tied to raising the incomes of these households through job creation.

FIGURE 10: Lived Poverty Index and Household Food Insecurity

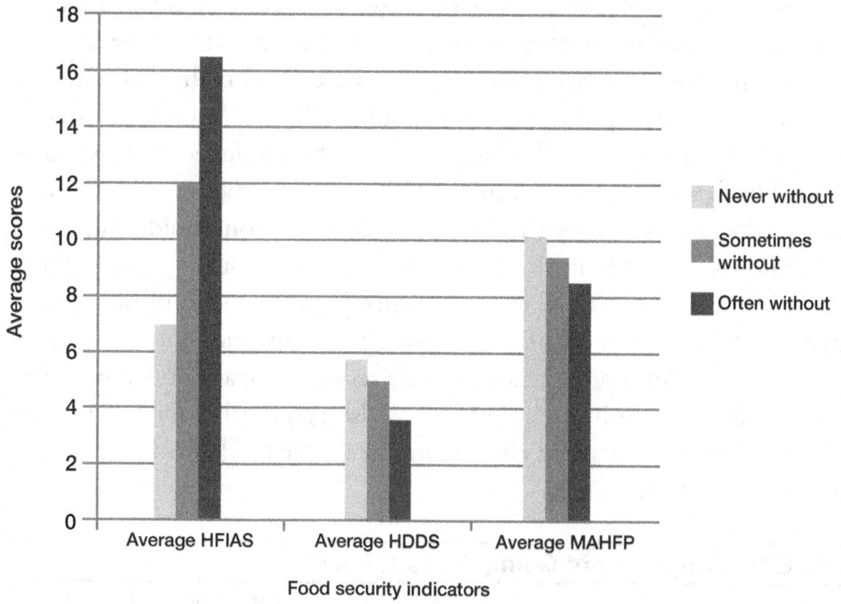

9. IMPACT OF FOOD PRICE INCREASES

There have been several studies of the impact of the global food crisis in 2007-2008 on food prices in Zambia and on urban consumers in particular.[56] These studies argue that the affordability of staple foods had been steadily improving in urban Zambia prior to the food price crisis.[57] Bread affordability increased steadily after the mid-1990s, as did maize grain from 2002 onwards. However, the spike in food prices during the food price crisis was a "major shock" to urban consumers and "reversed these gains in purchasing power, creating significant hardships for many urban households, especially the poor".[58] Purchasing power was lower in 2008/2009 than it had been in any year since 1994/1995.[59]

To understand the general impact of the food price crisis on poor households in Lusaka, the AFSUN survey first asked whether and how often they had gone without food in the previous six months due to food price increases. Only 5% of the households had never experienced food shortages (Table 16). Just over 11% said it was an everyday experience and 40% that it had happened more than once a week. A further 22% experienced food shortages on a weekly basis. In other words, food price increases had a strong and immediate impact on nearly two-thirds of all households.

Households were then asked which foods they had been forced to reduce or do without (Table 17). Price increases forced most households to consume less from every food group. The impact of price increases was felt most strongly in relation to cereals (where 79% of households had reduced their consumption) and meat/poultry (71%). Other food categories in which more than half the households had reduced consumption included fish (59%), roots and tubers (57%), dairy products (53%), fruit (52%) and sugar or honey (51%). While 80% of households had eaten some kind of vegetable in the 24 hours prior to the survey (see HDDS analysis above), 46% said they had reduced their consumption of vegetables in the previous month as a direct result of price increases. This suggests that the food price crisis not only reduced the absolute amount of food available to each household but was also responsible for a reduction in dietary diversity, possibly eliminating healthier foods from the diet of some households altogether.

TABLE 16: Frequency of Going Without Food		
	No.	%
Every day	43	11.5
More than once a week but less than every day	150	40.1
About once a week	82	21.9
About once a month	80	21.4
Never	19	5.1
	374	100.0

TABLE 17: Foods Gone Without Due to Price Increases		
	No.	%
Cereals (foods from grains)	280	79.1
Meat or poultry	251	70.7
Fresh or dried fish or shell fish	210	59.2
Roots or tubers	199	57.0
Cheese, yoghurt, milk or other milk products	189	53.2
Fruits	184	52.4
Sugars or honey	181	51.0
Foods made with oil, fat, or butter	173	48.7

10. Conclusions

The Lusaka urban food security survey shows that up to 93% of the households in the informal settlements, which house 75% of the population of the city, were food insecure, while a paltry 8% were food secure. Worse still, most of the households did not only have poor access to food, they also consumed foods from a very narrow range of food types. The majority of households (60%) consumed foods from no more than five food types out of a possible 12. Their diets were dominated by cereals, vegetables, sugar and other foods. The consumption of fruits, eggs, milk and milk products and even meat and poultry were low. Thus, the diets were likely to be deficient in essential vitamins, minerals and proteins. The survey therefore confirms that the Zambian diet is deficient in vitamins, iodine and iron and strongly supports the fortification of sugar and salt with vitamin A and iodine respectively. The survey also shows that the majority of households experienced chronic hunger, because they had hunger months ranging from 10 to 12 months. In fact, just 15% of the households surveyed had enough food throughout the year. Given the crucial role of food and adequate nutrition in the optimal functioning of the human body, and its essential role in social and economic development, the food insecurity situation in the surveyed areas of Lusaka is critical and requires urgent attention and specific measures to address it.

The economy of Zambia and the city of Lusaka have recently been buoyed by increased foreign direct investment and stable macro-economic conditions, including positive economic growth rates (averaging 6.5% since 2006) and a significant drop in inflation. Improved economic conditions in Lusaka are evident from the revival of the construction industry, growing investments in the manufacturing, wholesale and retail sectors, and the belated rehabilitation and provision of essential public infrastructure and services. Improvements in economic performance have yet to impact significantly on the backlog in public infrastructure and services, however. The Zambian urban housing deficit, for example, has been estimated at 3 million houses, while improved access to potable water and sanitation requires overhaul and expansion of the inadequate and dated water supply and the underdeveloped sanitation infrastructure.

Inadequate housing, water and sanitation infrastructure are compounded by a rapidly growing urban population from both natural increase and in-migration, especially into Lusaka. In consequence, an estimated 75% of the population of the city of Lusaka lives in compounds, high density housing areas initiated and developed largely by the city's low-income groups in response to the under-provision of housing by the municipal authorities and the government. Though the compounds house the majority of the city's population, they are the most inadequately serviced areas. The quality of housing in the compounds is mixed, with some good and many poorly-built houses adjacent to each other.

Access to potable water is poor and expensive, with some households forced to rely on water schemes developed mainly by NGOs with the support of international development agencies. Collection of solid waste is variable and in some cases non-existent, while sanitation is the perhaps the main challenge, as most households depend on shared pit latrines. These fill up quickly and inadequate space means new ones cannot be dug. A few houses rely on water-borne toilets linked to septic tanks, but the majority share pit latrines and some even make use of open spaces. Poor access to potable water and sanitation is worsened by high levels of poverty, which preclude some households from paying for the expensive safe water provided by NGOs and community groups in conjunction with the Lusaka Water and Sewerage Company. This is a company created out of the water and sewerage department of the Lusaka City Council in a bid to instill efficiency in the provision of water and sewerage services. It is wholly owned by the Lusaka City Council with a mandate to provide clean water supply and safe sanitation to the residents of the city.

Poverty levels in Lusaka remain high despite the economic improvements. Formal employment has been stagnant for years at just under 500,000 for Zambia as a whole and around 160,000 for the city of Lusaka. The low levels of formal employment in comparison to the size of the labour force (estimated at 750,000 in Lusaka) means that the bulk of the labour force tries to make a living in the unprotected informal sector. While wages in the formal sector are low in Lusaka and the rest of the country, they are higher than incomes in the informal sector. The sector is characterized by the absence of regulation or compliance with labour law, as well as low wages, particularly for those who do domestic work or are security guards and drivers.

Low wages in the formal and informal economies force many households to engage in multiple livelihoods to make ends meet. These include additional part-time work, small-scale trading and selling, piece work, renting out property or rooms and brewing beer for sale. Other common activities involve the provision of transport services (especially as unregistered passenger carriers and transporters of goods), wood and food processing, metal fabrication, tailoring, and mining and quarrying. There are also anti-social and illegal pursuits like prostitution, stealing and dealing in prohibited goods, drug trafficking and trading in game products including meat. An estimated 45% of the people engaged in informal economic activities in Lusaka are involved in trading. Intense competition in informal trading has reduced profit margins, resulting in low returns. While those with adequate capital still make worthwhile returns on their investments by taking advantage of volumes of sales, most people in informal trading are in it just to get by or survive. Survivalist informal businesses may help put food on the table, but have little growth potential.

The AFSUN Lusaka survey provides insights into the socio-economic characteristics of households in two adjacent low-income residential areas of Lusaka: Mandevu and Chipata Compounds. Only a quarter of the households surveyed earned income from the protected and better-paying formal sector, while the majority depend on income mainly from the unprotected informal sector. Most households earned low incomes but income inequality in the sample population was also high. The incomes of most households were so low that they could neither save nor remit to people outside the city. Most live a hand-to-mouth existence with their income paying for food, rent, utilities, education and health.

Households in these low-income residential areas of Lusaka experience chronic food insecurity. Only 15% of households had enough food to eat throughout the year. January and February were the only months when more than 50% of the households had enough to eat. Analysis of associations between food insecurity status and the socio-economic characteristics of households show that while food security status was related to variables like sex of the head of household, household structure and size of households and poverty status, income was the critical variable in urban household food security. This is because the households obtain their food mainly through the market and it is the amount of disposable income that largely determines household food security. This is confirmed by the response to food price increases in the year before the survey. Households reduced their consumption of all the food types, including cereals, and did without some food types completely.

Most of the households in the sample obtain their food from informal markets and small shops. The vast majority never obtain their food from the supermarkets and a surprising 97% reported that they produced no food through urban agriculture. This was largely due to the loss of land previously used for agricultural activities to housing and commercial developments. Most of the households were therefore dependent on the markets for their food. The low propensity to use supermarkets was related to households lacking the income to buy food in bulk. Instead, they bought food in small quantities on a daily basis as and when they earned some money from unstable informal economic activities.

The AFSUN survey shows that stable macro-economic conditions are critical to the food security of urban households, because these households obtain their food mainly through the market. Because food prices have tended to increase faster than wages, high inflation would adversely affect the food security of low-income urban households in terms of physical access to food, its dietary diversity and its adequacy over time. It is therefore critical to maintain stable macro-economic conditions that ensure that inflation remains low. Since urban household food security is positively associated with levels of income, promotion of decent employment is critical. Given the small proportion of low-income households in Lusaka earning income from the stable, better-paying formal sector and the depressed state of formal employment, the government needs to promote decent labour-intensive public works programmes to stimulate formal employment and boost household food security in the low-income urban areas.

Given the low educational attainment of the population in low-income urban settlements, the government ought to consider promoting literacy skills and providing programmes to help improve their productivity. Improved literacy and the possession of technical skills would improve the employment opportunities of the population in low-income households and enhance their food security status. Similarly, to increase school attendance, improve nutrition and raise the educational attainments of the children in low-income households, the government ought to expand the provision of school-based supplementary feeding programmes.[60] Furthermore, in view of the high levels of food insecurity in the low-income urban settlements, it is important that primary health care clinics provide supplementary feeding programmes for malnourished infants and children.[61]

ENDNOTES

1   J. Crush, B. Frayne and W. Pendleton, "The Crisis of Food Insecurity in African Cities" *Journal of Hunger & Environmental Nutrition* 7 (2-3) (2012): 271-92.

2   D. Satterthwaite, "The Under-Estimation of Urban Poverty in Low and Middle-Income Nations" IIED Poverty Reduction in Urban Areas Series No. 14, London, 2004; D. Mitlin and D. Satterthwaite, *Urban Poverty in the Global South: Scale and Nature* (London: Routledge, 2012).

3   D. Potts, "Counter-Urbanisation on the Zambian Copperbelt? Interpretations and Implications" *Urban Studies* 42 (2005): 583-609.

4   Central Statistics Office, *2010 Census of Population and Housing: Preliminary Report* (Lusaka, 2011), p. 3.

5   Ibid., p. 16.

6   D. Satterthwaite, G. McGranahan and C. Tacoli, "Urbanization and Its Implications for Food and Farming" *Philosophical Transactions of the Royal Society* 365 (2010): 2809-20.

7   D. Chiwele and R. Sikananu, "Agriculture Development and Food Security in Sub-Saharan Africa: Building a Case for More Support, A Case Study for Zambia" Report for FAO Agriculture Policy Analysis Unit, Rome, 2004.

8   N. Mason, W. Burke, A. Shipekesa and T. Jayne, "The 2011 Surplus in Smallholder Maize Production in Zambia: Drivers, Beneficiaries, and Implications for Agricultural and Poverty Reduction Policies" Working Paper No. 58, Food Security Research Project, Michigan State University, 2011.

9   P. Dorosh, S. Dradri and S. Haggblade, "Alternative Instruments for Ensuring Food Security and Price Stability in Zambia" Food Security Collaborative Working Papers 54488, Department of Agricultural, Food, and Resource Economics, Michigan State University, 2007; P. Dorosh, S. Dradri and S. Haggblade, "Regional Trade, Government Policy and Food Security: Recent Evidence from Zambia" *Food Policy* 34 (2009): 350-66.

10   K. Chimika Mwana, "The Political Economy of Food Security and Agriculture in Zambia" In R. Mkandawire and K. Matlosa, eds, *Food Policy and Agriculture in Southern Africa* (Harare: SAPES, 1993); J. Chizuni, "Food Policies and Food Security in Zambia" *Nordic Journal of African Studies* 3(1994): 46-52; V. Seshamani, "The Impact of Market Liberalisation on Food Security in Zambia" *Food Policy* 23 (1998): 539-51; N. Barratt, D. Chitundu, O. Dover, J. Elsinga, S. Eriksson, L. Guma, M. Haggblade, S. Haggblade, T. Henn, F. Locje, C. O'Donnell, C. Smith and T. Stevens "Cassava as Drought Insurance: Food Security Implications of Cassava Trials in Central Zambia" *Agregon* 45(2006): 106-23; N. Sitko, "Maize, Food Insecurity, and the Field of Performance in Southern Zambia" *Agriculture and Human Values* 25 (2008): 3-11; M. Hanjra and R. Culas, "The Political Economy of Maize Production and Poverty Reduction in Zambia: Analysis of the Last 50 Years" *Journal of Asian and African Studies* 46(2011): 546-66; S. Kodamaya, "Agricultural Policies and Food Security of Smallholder Farmers in Zambia" *African Study Monographs* S42 (2011): 19-39 and the numerous publications at http://fsg.afre.msu.edu/zambia/index.htm.

11   N. Mason and T. Jayne, "Staple Food Consumption Patterns in Urban Zambia: Results from the 2007/2008 Urban Consumption Survey" Working Paper No. 42, Food Security Research Project, Michigan State University, 2009.

12   G. Porter, T. Bowyer-Bower, D. Potts, F. Lyon, A. Adepetu, J. Olaniyan, H. Daloeng, C. Mulenga and S. Mumba, "Improving Market Institutions and Urban Food Supplies for the Urban Poor: A Comparative Study of Nigeria and Zambia" Report to DFID, London, 2004.

13   D. Lee-Smith, "Cities Feeding People: An Update on Urban Agriculture in Equatorial Africa" *Environment and Urbanization* 22(2010): 483-99; A. Zezza and L. Tascotti, "Urban Agriculture, Poverty and Food Security: Empirical Evidence from a Sample of Developing Countries" *Food Policy* 35(2010): 265-73; R. Stewart, M. Korth, L. Langer, S. Rafferty, N. Da Silva and C. van Rooyen, "What are the Impacts of Urban Agriculture Programs on Food Security in Low and Middle-Income Countries?" *Environmental Evidence* (2013): 2:7. D. Lee-Smith, "Which Way for UPA in Africa?" City 17 (2013): 369-84.

14   S. Bishwapriya, "Urban Agriculture: Who Cultivates and Why? A Case-Study of Lusaka, Zambia" *Food and Nutrition Bulletin* 7(1985): 15-24; C. Rakodi,

"Self Reliance or Survival? Food Production in African Cities with Particular Reference to Zambia" *African Urban Studies* 21(1985): 53-63; C. Rakodi, "Urban Agriculture: Research Questions and Zambian Evidence" *Journal of Modern African Studies* 26 (1988): 495-515; A. Drescher, "Urban Agriculture in the Seasonal Tropics: The Case of Lusaka, Zambia" In M. Koc, R. MacRae, L. Mougeot and J. Welsh, eds., *For Hunger-Proof Cities: Sustainable Urban Food Systems* (Ottawa: IDRC, 1999), pp. 67-76; D. Simatele and T. Binns, "Motivation and Marginalization in African Urban Agriculture: The Case of Lusaka, Zambia" *Urban Forum* 19(2008): 1-21; G. Hampwaye, "Decentralisation, Local Economic Development and Urban Agriculture in Zambia" PhD Thesis, University of Witwatersrand, 2008; D.Simatele, T. Binns and M. Simatele, "Sustaining Livelihoods under a Changing Climate: The Case of Urban Agriculture in Lusaka, Zambia" *Journal of Environmental Planning and Management* 55 (2012): 1175-91.

15   M. Hichaambwa, M. Beaver, A. Chapoto and M. Weber, "Patterns of Urban Food Consumption and Expenditure in Zambia" Working Paper No. 43, Food Security Research Project, Michigan State University, 2009, p. 63.

16   Ibid., pp. 86-8.

17   G. Hampwaye, E. Nel and C. Rogerson, "Urban Agriculture as Local Initiative in Lusaka, Zambia" *Environment and Planning C: Government and Policy* 25(2007): 553-72; A. Thornton, E. Nel and G. Hampwaye, "Cultivating Kaunda's Plan for Self-Sufficiency: Is Urban Agriculture Finally Beginning to Receive Support in Zambia?" *Development Southern Africa* 27(4) (2010): 613-25; D.Simatele, T. Binns and M. Simatele, "Urban Livelihoods under a Changing Climate: Perspectives on Urban Agriculture and Planning in Lusaka, Zambia" *Journal of Human Development and Capabilities* 269-93.

18   J. Crush, A. Hovorka and D. Tevera, "Food Security in Southern African Cities: The Place of Urban Agriculture" *Progress in Development Studies* 11(2011): 285-305; Lee-Smith, "Which Way for UPA in Africa?"

19   D. Miller, "'Retail Renaissance' or Company Rhetoric: The Failed Partnership of a South African Corporation and Local Suppliers in Zambia" *Labour, Capital and Society* 41(2008): 35-55; D. Miller, "Food Frontiers in Zambia: Resistance and Partnership in Shoprite's Retail Empire" *At Issue Ezine* 8 (2008); D. Miller, E. Nel and G. Hampwaye, "Malls in Zambia: Racialised Retail Expansion and South African Foreign Investors in Zambia" *African Sociological Review* 12(2008): 35-54; C. Abrahams, "Transforming the Region: Supermarkets and the Local Food Economy" *African Affairs* 109(2010): 115-34.

20   M. Hichaambwa and D. Tschirley, "Zambia Horticultural Rapid Appraisal: Understanding the Domestic Value Chains of Fresh Fruits and Vegetables" Working Paper No. 17, Food Security Research Project, Michigan State University, 2006; H. Haantuba and J. de Graaf, "Linkages Between Smallholder Farmers and Supermarkets: Lessons from Zambia" In E. McCullough, P. Pingali and K. Stamoulis (eds), *The Transformation of Agriculture-Food Systems: Globalization, Supply Chains and Smallholder Farmers* (London: Earthscan, 2008), pp. 207-23; R. Emongor and J. Kirsten, "The Impact of South African Supermarkets on Agricultural Development in the SADC: A Case Study in Zambia, Namibia and Botswana" *Agrekon* 48(2009): 60-84; M. Mwiinga, "An Assessment of Tomato Price Variability in Lusaka and Its Effects on Smallholder Farmers" MSc Thesis, Michigan State University, 2009.

21   D. Weatherspoon and T. Reardon, "The Rise of Supermarkets in Africa:

Implications for Agrifood Systems and the Rural Poor" *Development Policy Review* 21 (2003): 333-55.

22   J. Crush and B. Frayne, "Supermarket Expansion and the Informal Food Economy in Southern African Cities: Implications for Urban Food Security" *Journal of Southern African Studies* 37 (2011): 781-807.

23   Abrahams, "Transforming the Region: Supermarkets and the Local Food Economy."

24   N. Mason and T. Jayne, "Staple Food Consumption Patterns in Urban Zambia: Results from the 2007/2008 Urban Consumption Survey" Working Paper No. 36, Food Security Research Project, Michigan State University, 2009, p. 3.

25   M. Hichaambwa, "Urban Consumption Patterns of Livestock Products in Zambia and Implications for Policy" Working Paper No. 65, Food Security Research Project, Michigan State University, 2011, p. 6.

26   J. Collins, "Lusaka: the Historical Development of a Planned Capital, 1931-1970" In G. Williams, ed., *Lusaka and Its Environs: A Geographical Study of a Planned Capital City in Tropical Africa* (Lusaka: Associated Printer, 1986).

27   A. Chilivumbo and N. Mijere, "Rural-Urban Migration and Urbanisation in Zambia During the Colonial and Post-Colonial Periods" In E. Kalipeni, ed., *Population Growth and Environmental Degradation in Southern Africa* (Colorado: Lynne Rienner, 1994); E. Mutale, *The Management of Urban Development in Zambia* (Aldershot: Gower 2004).

28   J. Sutton and G. Langmead, *An Enterprise Map of Zambia* (London: International Growth Centre, 2013), pp. 6-10.

29   P. Carmody, "An Asian-Driven Economic Recovery in Africa? The Zambian Case" *World Development* 37 (2009): 1197-207; P. Carmody and G. Hampwaye, " Inclusive or Exclusive Globalization?: Zambia's Economy and Asian Investment" *Africa Today* 56 (2010):. 84-102; P. Kragelund and G. Hampwaye, "Seeking Markets and Resources: State-Driven Chinese and Indian Investments in Zambia" *International Journal of Technology and Globalisation* 6(2012): 352-68.

30   A. Legge, J. Orchard, A. Graffham, P. Greenhalgh and U. Kleih, "The Production of Fresh Produce in Africa for Export to the United Kingdom: Mapping Different Value Chains" Natural Resources Institute, 2006, p. 77.

31   S. Sasaki, H. Suzuki, Y. Fujino, Y. Kimura, and M. Cheelo, "Impact of Drainage Networks on Cholera Outbreaks in Lusaka, Zambia" *American Journal of Public Health* 99(2009): 1982-7; M. Fernández, A. Bauernfeind, J. Jiménez, C. Gil, N. El Omeiri and D. Guibert, "Influence of Temperature and Rainfall on the Evolution of Cholera Epidemics in Lusaka, Zambia, 2003-2006: Analysis of a Time Series" *Transactions of the Royal Society of Tropical Medicine & Hygiene* 103(2009): 137-43; A. Irena, M. Mwambazi and V. Mulenga, "Diarrhea is a Major Killer of Children with Severe Acute Malnutrition Admitted to Inpatient Set-up in Lusaka, Zambia" *Nutrition Journal* (2011): 10:110.

32   K. Hansen, "The Informalization of Lusaka's Economy: Regime Change, Ultra-Modern Markets and Street Vending, 1972-2004" In J-B. Gewald, M. Hinfelaar and G. Macola, eds., *One Zambia, Many Histories: Towards a History of Post-Colonial Zambia* (Leiden: J. Brill, 2008), pp. 213-39.

33   K. Hansen, "Changing Youth Dynamics in Lusaka's Informal Economy in the Context of Economic Liberalization" *African Studies Quarterly* 11(2010): 13-27; P. Ndhlovu, "Street Vending in Zambia: A Case of Lusaka District" MA in

Development Studies, ISS, The Hague, 2011; M. Shaha, "The Informal Economy of Zambia: Can it Disappear? Should it Disappear?" Working Paper 12/0425, International Growth Centre, London, 2013.

34   K. Hansen, "Who Rules the Streets? The Politics of Vending Space in Lusaka" In K. Hansen and M. Vaa, eds., *Reconsidering Informality: Perspectives from Urban Africa* (Uppsala: Nordic Africa Institute, 2004), pp. 62-80; W. Nchito, "Formalising Trading Places and Spaces: An Analysis of the Informal Sector in Lusaka, Zambia" in D. Banik, ed., *The Legal Empowerment Agenda: Poverty, Labour and the Informal Economy in Africa* (London: Ashgate, 2011), pp. 87-106.

35   K. Hansen, *Salaula: The World of Secondhand Clothing and Zambia* (Chicago: University of Chicago Press, 2000).

36   W. Nchito and K. Hansen, "Passport Please: The Cross-Border Traders Association in Zambia" In I. Lindell, ed., *Africa's Informal Workers. Collective Agency, Alliances and Transnational Organizing in Urban Africa* (London: Zed Press, 2010).

37   T. McNamee, "A Study of Chinese Traders in South Africa, Lesotho, Botswana, Zambia and Angola" Discussion Paper 2012/03, Brenthurst Foundation, Johannesburg, 2012.

38   The 2007/2008 Urban Consumption Survey (UCS) found that households in Lusaka spent 47% of their total expenditures on food. However, households in the lowest two income quintiles spent as much as 60% of their income on food; see Mason and Jayne, "Staple Food Consumption Patterns in Urban Zambia" p. 7.

39   Mason and Jayne, "Staple Food Consumption Patterns in Urban Zambia."

40   Hichaambwa, "Urban Consumption Patterns of Livestock Products."

41   B. Frayne, "Pathways of Food: Mobility and Food Transfers in Southern African Cities" *International Development Planning Review* 32(2010): 291-310.

42   J. Harris , P. Kelly and S. Filteau, "Interactions Between HIV, Dietary Diversity and Socioeconomic Position in an Urban African Setting" *Medical Journal of Zambia* 37(2010): 180-5.

43   P. Dorosh, P. Dradri and S. Haggblade, "Regional Trade and Food Security: Recent Evidence from Zambia" In A. Sarris and J. Morrison, eds, *Food Security in Africa: Market and Trade Policy for Staple Foods in Eastern and Southern Africa* (Cheltenham: Edward Elgar, 2010), pp. 180-220.

44   L. Mukata, "Nutrition of Children and Adults" In *Zambia Demographic and Health Survey 2007* (Lusaka: Central Statistical Office, 2009), pp. 155-76.

45   See http://www.ers.usda.gov/topics/food-nutrition-assistance/food-security-in-the-us/measurement.aspx#.UeleDI21HYQ.

46   P. Pinstrup-Andersen, "Food Security: Definition and Measurement" *Food Security* 1(2009): 5-7; C. Barrett, "Measuring Food Insecurity" *Science* 327 (2010): 825-8; A. Renhazo and D. Mellor, "Food Security Measurement in Cultural Pluralism: Missing the Point or Conceptual Misunderstanding?" *Nutrition* 26(2010): 1-9; D. Headey and O. Ecker, "Improving the Measurement of Food Security" IFPRI Discussion Paper No. 01225, Washington DC, 2012.

47   J. Coates, A. Swindale and P. Bilinsky, "Household Food Insecurity Access Scale (HFIAS) for Measurement of Food Access: Indicator Guide (Version 3)" Food and Nutrition Technical Assistance Project, Academy for Educational Development, Washington DC, 2007.

48   A. Swindale and P. Bilinsky, "Household Dietary Diversity Score (HDDS) for

Measurement of Household Food Access: Indicator Guide (Version 2)" Food and Nutrition Technical Assistance Project, Academy for Educational Development, Washington DC, 2006.

49 P. Bilinsky and A. Swindale, "Months of Adequate Household Food Provisioning (MAHFP) for Measurement of Household Food Access: Indicator Guide" Food and Nutrition Technical Assistance Project, Academy for Educational Development, Washington DC, 2007.

50 B. Frayne et al, *The State of Urban Food Insecurity in Southern Africa*, AFSUN Urban Food Security Series No. 2, Cape Town, 2010.

51 J. Harris and S. Drimie, " Toward an Integrated Approach for Addressing Malnutrition in Zambia: A Literature Review and Institutional Analysis" IFPRI Discussion Paper No. 01200, Washington DC, 2012.

52 A. Richards, *Land, Labour and Diet in Northern Rhodesia* (London: James Currey, 1939; reprinted 1995); H. Moore and M. Vaughan, *Cutting Down Trees: Gender, Nutrition and Change in the Northern Province of Zambia, 1890-1990* (New York: Heinemann 1994).

53 Central Statistics Office, *Living Conditions Monitoring Survey Reports, 2004, 2006 and 2009*, Lusaka.

54 M. Chibuye, "Interrogating Urban Poverty Lines: The Case of Zambia" Human Settlements Working Paper Series No. 30, IIED, London, 2011.

55 R. Mattes, "The Material and Political Bases of Lived Poverty in Africa: Insights from the Afrobarometer" In V. Moller, D. Huschka and A. Michalos, eds., *Barometers of Quality of Life Around the Globe* (Rueil-Malmaison: Springer Science & Business Media, 2008), pp. 161-85.

56 N. Mason, T. Jayne, C. Donovan and A. Chapoto, "Are Staple Foods Becoming More Expensive for Urban Consumers in Eastern and Southern Africa? Trends in Food Prices, Marketing Margins and Wage Rates in Kenya, Malawi, Mozambique and Zambia" In D. Lee and M. Ndulo, eds, *The Food and Financial Crises in Sub-Saharan Africa: Origins, Impacts and Policy Implications* (Cambridge, Mass: CABI, 2011), pp. 154-88; N. Mason, T. Jayne, A. Chapoto and C. Donovan, "Putting the 2007/2008 Global Food Crisis in Longer-Term Perspective: Trends in Staple Food Affordability in Urban Zambia and Kenya" *Food Policy* 26(2011): 350-67.

57 Mason, Jayne, Chapoto and Donovan, "Putting the 2007/2008 Global Food Crisis in Longer-Term Perspective" p. 351.

58 Ibid., pp. 355, 362.

59 Ibid., p. 356.

60 In June 2013, the Government announced that it planned to widen its school feeding programme as only a quarter of vulnerable children nationwide were covered by the existing programme; see "School Feeding Programme" *Zambian Economist* 11 June 2013.

61 B. Amadi, M. Mwiya, E. Chomba, M. Thomson, C. Chintu, P. Kelly and J. Walker-Smith, "Improved Nutritional Recovery on an Elemental Diet in Zambian Children with Persistent Diarrhoea and Malnutrition" *Journal of Tropical Pediatrics* 51(2005): 5-10.

Printed in the United States
By Bookmasters